T0244731

# Malak

AKRON SERIES IN POETRY

# Malak

Jenny Sadre-Orafai

The University of Akron Press
Akron, Ohio

ISBN: 978-1-62922-291-2 (paper)
ISBN: 978-1-62922-292-9 (ePDF)
ISBN: 978-1-62922-293-6 (ePub)

A catalog record for this title is available from the Library of Congress.

∞ The paper used in this publication meets the minimum requirements of ANSI/NISO
z39.48–1992 (Permanence of Paper).

Cover image: Arghavan Khosravi, *At Her Fingertips*. Cover design by Amy Freels.

*Malak* was designed and typeset in Minion with Helvetica titles by Amy Freels and printed on
sixty-pound natural.

Produced in conjunction with the University of
Akron Affordable Learning Initiative.
More information is available at
www.uakron.edu/affordablelearning/.

*for Haj Khanoom*


*for Nate and for Bella*

# Contents

# Burning in a Hot Moon

*I was born to a dying moon, a dead room. You were born
to a hot moon, a burnt view.* What moons do

before we're alive is up to them. This moon is seven days
old. Malak draws a house on a house wall. *Here's you,*

*your room, crickets for luck—jumping in your closet.* I draw fire
on windows. I swallow the air and down each kite.

# Mouthing the Future

My father tells me to not tell my friends.
*They won't believe your grandmother sees*

*patterns divide, gold fields in coffee, a fox tail*
*twitching in the seam where the handle*

*meets the cup.* I believe so hard that I write
down her language, residue. Who will tell us

what happens after she's gone?
*Don't put that future in my mouth—I can't say it.*

# Chirology

When we sent you out for fire,
you brought back ash. White
palm bones flood black film,
we thought you'd see
the rind, the shine your body makes.
We thought you must have changed
your path, disrupted lines to a future
now gone ghost. We thought you must
have seen yourself being robbed
of the first and second wives, both
brunette, of twin and identical boys
with their mother's eyes, of the house
with two chimneys and five identical doors,
then, of that terrific sun that comes before
the house is blown apart by storm.

# Forecasting

Gulps of gray crown
an exhausted sky.
On the other side,
we are safe, away with
crickets who sing
without pause. To see
a storm approach
someone and not call
is pulling a ladder away,
is readying your ears
for the blast.

# How They Arrive

They carry cups like newborns to her,
careful with all their hope.

She points at coffee grounds:
bags of money in houses

and mouths filled with straight teeth.
A woman who couldn't read

taught Malak how when she was young,
when she didn't know how much people

needed to be told what was coming.
A snake with its jaw hinge slack.

# Path to the Split Log Home

Our cloudbursts sing,
*Most are welcome!*

Our planting is dictated
by the zodiac.

Our trapdoors lead
to sweet potatoes.

Our earth is wild—
horseradish, boneset, peppermint.

Our baby girls and boys
wear dresses.

Our mothers step on infant hems,
keep them from harm.

Our trees can only be killed
after we cut rings around them.

Our first frost means
now we kill the hogs.

Our sheep distrust
wanderers in pants.

Our snakes won't die
until sundown.

The sisters ask that you leave
the same door you entered.

# Lots, Enormous Spaces

She's translating what hasn't happened yet.
She isn't inventing it. I can't speak

her language, so her son translates
the translation. Even when

she's speaking the present it sounds like
she's talking the future.

She uses her free hand to tell me lots
of weddings or lots of money or I will meet

the short man who will buy me lots
of presents. Lots of everything.

Lots, enormous spaces, where gloom waits
for her to turn the cup back over.

## Hearing Secrets

Hold the beginning in a hand.
Remove what's missing,

vowels that will save you.
Broken emblems are gestures

on faces posing for love or food or money.
Lean away from what you remember.

Nod until a twin life lands
in another hand.

# Autobiography at Fifty Feet

We'll write our autobiography when we're teenagers,
before we grow into our teeth. Before we meet
people who will laugh at us for reasons we'll talk about
when we're older and divorced. And we'll both still know
our exes because we have to, not because we want to.
We'll write our autobiography just before we kiss
in the log flume tunnel, our log smacking against the rail,
and we'll pretend, for that part of the ride, we're old.
We'll write that I squirmed next to you when you said
there were snakes and that they'd launch themselves
like canned confetti into our log that wasn't really a log
of course, and that the kids, somewhere behind us, said
the water smelled like urine. We'll tell everyone
our teeth glowed in that darkness when we laughed.

# Company

Malak hears futures in cups the way we hear oceans
inside shells. Families we know rush through
Turkish coffee, scalding their throats. They wear
black stripes down their tongues like garter snakes,
leave enough to drip when propped against
the saucer. We exchange the quiet of living. Waiting
until the inside dries, until it stops drawing.

# Wearing It Out

The other grandmother wore a shot fox across her shoulders.
I petted its paws when she visited the grocery store.

There were so many looks. The fox's eyes stuck open,
looking back. Children tugged parents in aisles.

A sleeper bag hung, waiting for it to return. I thought
at least the fox has its own room and its own eyes.

I'd knock and ask it to play. I don't know why she took it out
so much, all that dying waiting to take her.

## Last Reading

There's a pregnant bird in the cup.
Malak looks at me like she's never looked

at that in a cup before. My father looks at me
like there're things I'm not telling him.

She crochets baby caps, square blankets,
booties in Neapolitan ice cream colors.

If I ever have these babies, if I'm the bird
in the cup, I'll want to devour them.

After the last reading, she leaves the cup turned up,
daring the bird to forget I am pregnant.

# Queen of Cups

Queen Elizabeth was with Philip in Kenya
when her father died. She was watching

elephants from a hotel within the trees.
My father was with his three sisters

when his mother died. I was with my bed,
hallucinating a fox. After the fox left,

I called him, but he was taking a shower.
Like a movie, the protagonist crying

surrounded by water, lots of empty cups?
Was Elizabeth instructed to not cry?

*It will shake this tree.*
*The elephants will trample this nest.*

# Karaj

When I miss her, I open my popout map. Spilling my face
into Tehran streets, I hide in Laleh Park. I read street names
aloud like I'm reporting to someone. I pretend to see things
no one else can—who took the Peacock throne, how
the burnt city fell. I say *Karaj* like I'm telling the future.

# You Will Meet a Man

I stood on him,
a well of dirt
that mends,

and breathed in
his boyhood, what's left
of air in altitude.

I could recite
every line on his hand,
behind his ears.

Should I tell it—
we will live
against a knife that

your mother,
a girl, watched
sharpen, wane, and then

a flat line.

# Call and Response

Nine ladders is the dream that keeps
coming—its back with kites, all diamonds,

between the rungs. The ninth dream
is nine ladders with bows at their necks,

diamonds in their ears, and violet sandals
climbing every rung. Nine times nine ladders

that go nowhere, no back to waking up
in cups that can't speak.

# A Break and a Fracture

*Break*

The sun falling made the bone yellow then pink
then black. I left it there. Had I brought it to her,

she would touch my tooth whole, cover the empty
space in a girl's mouth.

*Fracture*

I fell down concrete stairs, landed on elbow or wing.
Her son's hands and working elbows fastened hair away

from my face, his daughter, each morning. Have you seen
the sad film that she's left over us?

Have you watched bone knit itself together like the future?

II

# The Present

I made the door lock without a key, once without a
hand. I like to think that it came from Malak and
not the woman at the food co-op. My grandmother
and I wore the same shoe size, wore the same small
bird shoulders too. The woman at the store says,
*We looked alike when I was younger.* Her hair looks
like it's been bleached in a bathroom, and cut there,
too. I nod when she tells me, *You're like my twin.*
Nodding is the polite thing to do when we have
different color eyes.

If I concentrate hard on something, I can make it happen—car glass shattering, radios shutting down, computers going dark. I've never known an actual lumberjack, but I wrote the word *lumberjack* once. Twice now. I didn't tell anyone. I went to school the next day, and in my classroom, a fortune left from someone's cookie. In red: *The lumberjack must always keep a sharp ax.* I carried the paper with me until it wasn't there anymore.

I dated a man who wore a spear through his ear cartilage, helix to lobe. It flashed when he told me to not be afraid of everything that blinked around me. *It's reassurance you're exactly where you should be.* He explained numbers and Japanese superstitions and things I can't recall because they don't matter anymore.

I like looking at pictures of identical twins or I like pretending that someone's given me two pictures and I have to spot the differences. I look at Malak sometimes like she's my twin or I search her face for the pieces I can't see in mine.

I locked the bedroom door without realizing. I felt like I was in a cave, and I needed him to throw more light than he could. We painted the outside of the house in neons like the eighties. It didn't swell into the room fast enough. There was no husband to shine my way out. My hands didn't turn the lock.

I can't tell you how to walk on agony, on defeat. Oh, there's no trouble in this song. Why shouldn't we be brave in the light of everything flashing? Drop your walk. Run in every road. Forget sleeping for weeks. Today, I tried to wipe a crumb from my pants, but it was the sun.

My other grandmother was kept on a farm and tried to convince the circus to take her. At night, her dad came for her, followed big animal noises in fields. Maybe she had magic in her own green eyes. I never saw it. She wasn't like Malak with bird shoulders and hands that were wrinkled even when she was young.

Raw quartz is rock candy disguised as broken caves, makes me sleep like I can't stop. I take every amethyst and trade it for rubies. They don't bring sleep. Their red is loud and her favorite. I pack them into the pillowcase. She'll come back for the nest.

The right rear tire of the car in front of me will burst. Both hands on the wheel like my father taught me in a high school parking lot, like all fathers. I won't move from the tire's path. I'm daring it to do what I tell it. Several minutes later, the tire blows. I know and I swerve.

III

# When I'm Just Dead

I'll send a fox to my daughter. It will nest in her hair,
my heaviest sleeping girl—largest heart outside my body.

She will shove it aside, look for me in a tin box
of necklaces I circled her with when she was a cricket.

She'll drink water from a bottle too tight at the lip.
She'll draw my face on the wall and tell it everything.

# We Can't Change the Orbits Quite Yet

We have long talks about
what color my blood really is,

how many hearts the octopus can
make breath and still swim with.

I think the Hudson is the river
and not the dog. I want the shoulder

and muscles, the muzzle to be a rounded
wave. We can make it make sense.

Here's the octopus, three hearts
beating in the mantle.

Here's my open finger
and my red blood.

Here's a man walking his pressed shirt
down the rainy street anyway.

Here's the muscle in his jaw moving
up and down, a seesaw.

Here's his shoulder pushing
out of your wave and into

a message from my mother
in pictures. She's past words

now, and I hear everything
she means. The sound

of a small plane in the suburban sky
is my father saying hello.

# Lucy Let People See

I'm alone in the back of a cab.
The driver tells me about the Awash
and Lucy's bones. He talks about them
like how I talk about futures. *Lucy let people see.*
His hands are the longest I've ever seen.
I think of what his skeleton must look like—
languid, slippery. We talk about languages
we know, how many other ways we could be
having this conversation. He takes me through
a tunnel that reminds me of a cave, a depression.

# Markers

First coyote

First big rock

First pink sky

First bruise

First fork

First well water

First cricket

First spell

First fast

First shadow

First villain

First fire

First no

# Frequency Interference

My ears ring when an airplane's
in the next town.

Call it frequency. Call it
magic. Invisible headphones
with singing bells.

Should I push my wings
out too? Carry the crying
babies behind my teeth?

It's true that Malak's a white plane
on a white cloud, reading
land, laughing at winking
rivers, waiting for me to turn

gold, gold, gold, gold.

# Telegraph

I learn two words in sign language.
*Heaven* and *heel.* They're side by side.

If I run into the fox again, I'll tell her *heel,*
like you tell a tame animal.

I will tell her where to put the grandmother
she took. And I will keep a look out.

# Round Lake Yearbook

The way you know the day is by getting mad
at the stars, the chickens, the lists,
at the noisemakers mostly.

The way you know what time it is
is by reading glow-in-the-dark stickers
on an overhead fan that belonged to your teenage self.

The way you predict the future and don't tell anyone
is the same way you know you will ruin every manicure
on purpose by eating pistachios.

The way you carefully pass a school bus
with a sign across the back: *DRIVER IN TRAINING.*
The way the phrase fits the situation.

The way we don't have to be this loud when we're old.
Our bones are good news. They heal on their own.
Our bones are the best things to keep us standing.

The way, when I mentioned your name, all the rabbits
and hares came out of the forest and smelled
a different air, their whiskers trembling.

The way your hairline falls into my face
and every dream happens again but on different roads,
and you put me in my grave and you see it.

The way other people I can't think of right now
don't make us sisters with so many dreams,
with so many windows open or let down.

The way we handle the life and death of public art.
The way we tell the mural good news,
bad news, how it's still in need of urgent care.

The way that man who lived five miles away
was a gunman, how we gave money
for their funerals in Wisconsin.

The way we tell the cicadas to please hit more notes.
The way the new finch doesn't know space.
The way we fall into place around Round Lake.

The way no one here is awake yet.
The way we raise the dead is real.
Our whole gold life is happening.

# We Buried the Fathers in Northville

Air pours out of a defeated tire on the highway.
We point. We say *ghost*. There goes the rim
sparking, a firecracker.

And when we see the windmill next
to the barn on some small road,
we say, *Michigan, you don't know how to look*

*real*. Your trees are stretched gold coins
pulled from a top hat.
You make our mouths miss the dead.

We know somebody's dad will walk out
to the square with its bumpy sidewalks,
shake his pockets clean for pebbles, push them

inside his leather shoes. He will suffer
for our suffering as long as it hurts. Surely,
we can stop the windmill if we want harder.

# Listen

We found the first bird behind the museum near Sixteenth.
We held hands, and it wasn't vulgar until we were standing

at a funeral. Yes, I let go first. My wings pulled in tight.
Death is the most comfortable suit.

And I wanted to take its picture like the bird was going off
to its first day of school.

I wanted to pick it up, put it in the front seat, drive it
back home. I wanted you to say something.

The second bird sounded like a baseball hitting
my bedroom window, somebody's best arm pitching.

But it was a flat cloud of oil and down. Listen, that's two.
Their song is here, and I can't put it back into their mouths.

It's autumn, and it's in the trees that look like fire.
The birds listen, even after dark.

# Mother Spell

I felt for mountain
and ocean, my first globe.

Mouth or beak. Arm or wing.
Skin or feather. Feet or feet.

Who brought these to me
to dress in booties and caps.

I didn't ask to know a belly
so tight.

I didn't ask if it was girl
or boy or bird.

# Jamshid's Angoor

In the spring I'm at my childhood home.
My father goes to and from the store
with dark grapes for his daughter.

He holds them by the tops
of their heads to the sink, drops
them in a bowl. Dunking them,

he pulls them out like he's making
something more than grapes clean.
He's cautious with his hands like

he's a father of an infant again.
Like he's a father of an infant again
who makes her body go corpse

every time she hits water and then
waits for the attention, the calling,
the bringing her body back to life.

# I Saw You'd Be Born

A rainbow shadow
lapping around you.
You'd take time
with nature. I saw
your teeth come
crooked, canine.
You wouldn't bite
before you were bit.

# Gospel

You're still running from the chain
letter you didn't write because you saw

your life would be safe, miraculous.
Your apartment filled with balloons

bobbing, shoving their way into ceilings
and, if only, the sky. The person you love

most doesn't live with you but loves you
more than her hair that made its way

into your undying succulent farm. So still
with your trunk, your arms, your legs when

you lie down because the streamers in
the blow of the heat are telling you

something you don't know yet,
and you call it truth.

# Piloting

Draw a breath into the pit of a hand.
Tell the rabbit to drink there. Give

its heart slowness. What's left to scare
from. Wash its face, its thrumming

feet lucky. Open your mouth, carry
it to the next place, out of past,

present. Say, *Here's your deepest sleep.*

# Lifecasting

I stood for it, and the plaster felt like
the raw egg we wore on our tight,

tight pores. (We slipped the yellows,
full suns, down the sink.)

He demolded me after I read him
his hand. I said, *Pick one*, from the pile

of parts. He pulled my other head, blank.
My other body, an empty piñata,

held up a wall. His hand over
that mouth means nothing.

# Language of Signs

I slept the whole day
without remembering, Malak.

I dreamt I had a son
growing so fast,

a tomato plant sprawled
everywhere, unstoppable.

I held him at my hipline.
And I fed his hunger.

Now he's a pitcher
of water.

His teeth hiding
behind his father's lips,

or proud outside
of his mouth, like mine.

Then, Malak, I saw a nun,
a black veil trailed her head.

And I followed her like a ghost
or bride.

Who has my voice?
Let me follow it.

# Blank Nature

Dents in a window pause
at thunder and cross this
quiet horse. Draw him afraid
of an audience or that
best stable overrun with
hay and bridles and carrots
and tails swaying to what.
Then let him graze.

\*\*\*

I don't have to tell you
that uncooked yolks
in the sunlight always
cancel each other out.
Practice scale. Now
suffering. Finally, heal.

You must drive a machine
to freedom. Its purpose
dissolves under foot.
*Take back the factories*,
I say. Rush into them
and rescue the workers.

\*\*\*

Conduct a wetless
seashore, no more
suffering. No more
tight water. We aren't
up to our necks
in the charge.

You are a coat on water,
your own exhibit.

Your rabbit heart is a prayer.

Blank nature is something
to steal, how you know fear.

\*\*\*

Electric, you are the certain
vice, the important hands
that will invite the talking.

Your daughter is
your daughter because
she calls you
mother deer.

\*\*\*

A blank picture
of a fire burning
is just broken bones.

A blank sound
when your daughter sees
a chick hatch from an egg
for the first time, her open
mouth cried
nothing.

\*\*\*

A blank body
when somebody
grabs at your coat again.
You reach for the wool hem,
*This belongs to me.*

# Acknowledgments

I am very grateful to the editors of the following journals where these poems first appeared, at times as earlier versions.

*The Bakery*: "Chirology"

*The Collapsar*: "Forecasting," "Markers," and "You Will Meet a Man"

*Dialogist*: "Blank Nature"

*Los Angeles Review*: "It Came From" ("The Present")

*MiPOesias*: "Yearbook of Ways" ("Round Lake Yearbook")

*Mount Hope*: "Where You Were" ("Queen of Cups")

*Ninth Letter*: "Language of Signs" and "We Buried the Fathers in Northville"

*PANK*: "Biography of Teenagers" ("Autobiography at Fifty Feet")

*Poemeleon*: "Lucy Let People See"

*Redivider*: "Listen"

*RHINO*: "After the Hard Part Comes the Future" ("Company," "How They Arrive," "Lots, Enormous Spaces," and "Mouthing the Future")

*Tammy*: "We Can't Change the Orbits Quite Yet"

*Thrush Poetry Journal*: "Karaj"

I'm very grateful to Mary Biddinger for inviting me to be a part of The University of Akron Press again. Thank you to Jon and Amy at the press for their support. Gratitude to Arghavan Khosravi for the cover art, *At Her Fingertips*.

Thank you always to my parents, my sister, Nate, and Bella. I want to thank Michelle and Peter at Platypus Press for seeing *Malak* and giving the book its first home. Thank you to Komal for all of it. Rebecca, thank you for pushing me to write when I don't want to and when I don't believe I can. Heaps of love to Jennifer K. Sweeney for the keenest eye and biggest heart. I am beyond grateful to Airea D. Matthews and Wendy C. Ortiz for their brilliance and kindness. Thank you to my teachers.

Jenny Sadre-Orafai is the author of *Paper Cotton Leather*, *Malak*, and *Dear Outsiders* and is the coauthor of *Book of Levitations*. Her prose has appeared in *The Rumpus*, *Fourteen Hills*, *The Los Angeles Review*, *The Collagist*, and others. She cofounded and coedits *Josephine Quarterly* and teaches creative writing at Kennesaw State University.

Printed in the United States
by Baker & Taylor Publisher Services